A Quick Reference to

THE

RESEARCH

PAPER

Sharon Sorenson

AMSCO SCHOOL PUBLICATIONS, INC.
315 Hudson Street
New York, NY 10013

Design: Text and Cover, Merrill Haber

Compositor and artwork: ECL

When ordering this book, please specify: **R 596 P** *or*
A QUICK REFERENCE TO THE RESEARCH PAPER

ISBN 1-56765-052-x
NYC Item 56765-052-9

5 6 7 8 9 10   02 01 00 99

Contents

Introduction

Here is a simple, easy-to-follow twelve-step guide for writing a research paper. The assignment to do a "research paper" may come under several labels.

Report

A report is usually a summary of only one or two sources that develops a topic but not a thesis.

Factual research paper

A factual research paper is an expanded report using multiple sources but still developing only a topic, not a thesis.

Evaluative research paper

Most often teachers want an evaluative research paper, one that is developed from multiple sources but addresses problem-solutions, causes or effects, comparisons or contrasts, assessment, analysis, or interpretation. It supports a topic and a thesis and may reach a conclusion that expresses an opinion.

Term paper

A term paper is a paper written for a specific course during a specific semester—or term. The term paper can be anything from a simple report to an evaluative research paper. Clarify what is expected of you.

For any research assignment, be sure you understand the purpose and audience for your final product.

STEP 1: BEGIN WITH A PLAN

Once you understand your assignment, before you lift a pen or head for the library, plan your work. Use the Time-Management Chart to plot your work on a calendar. Then stick to your plan to make sure you finish on schedule.

STEP 2: CHOOSE A TOPIC

Your broad subject may be assigned. Even if it is, chances are you will need to narrow it to a manageable topic for the space and time you have to work. On the other hand, you may have to choose your own topic. For topic ideas, consult the daily media—radio, television, newspapers, the Internet. Consider your school, work, and personal interests. Listen carefully to general conversations, for they, too, may suggest topics. Choose a topic that's right for you and for your assignment.

Time Management Chart

Weeks until final draft is due	10	8	6	4
Number of days to complete:				
Choosing a topic (Step 2)	4	3	2	1
Preliminary work (Step 3)	4	3	2	1
Secondary references (Step 4)	5	4	3	2
Bibliography cards (Step 5)	1	1	1	1
Primary references (Step 6)	5	4	3	2
Note taking (Step 7)	10	8	6	4
Final Outline (Step 8)	1	1	1	1
Drafting (Step 9)	9	7	5	3
Revising (Step 10)	4	3	3	2
Final Draft (Step 11)	6	5	4	3
Proofreading (Step 12)	1	1	1	1

Choose a good topic that has these characteristics:

Interesting A good topic holds your interest and that of your audience; it's something you want to learn more about.

Manageable You have only a limited amount of time and resources available, so choose a topic you can handle.

Worthwhile Choose something of substance, something that matters.

Original A good topic is not just a rehashing, for instance, of Abraham Lincoln's childhood. A more original topic might be how the books he read as a boy seem to have influenced his later political decisions.

Avoid a poor topic with these characteristics:

Too broad Avoid a topic which is too broad. The Ice Age is far too broad a topic, but the role of the Ice Age in the formation of the Great Lakes will work. Hieroglyphics is too broad a topic, but how original Egyptian hieroglyphics are protected will work.

Too narrow By contrast, also avoid a topic which is too narrow, one for which little information is available. For example, metric cooking conversions is too narrow; it can be explained in a few sentences or even in a chart. The complexity of national metric conversion, however, has sufficient breadth for a suitable topic.

Avoid a topic that is:

Too trivial Every driver's manual, for example, will name the same laws of the road, so the topic is too trivial.

Too subjective You must set personal preferences aside to respond objectively to a research topic.

Too controversial Hotly contested arguments can bog you down—remember the part about being an objective researcher.

Too familiar You face boredom and will likely forget your audience's unfamiliarity with your topic.

Too technical Doing the research will keep you busy enough without your having to simultaneously learn a technical language.

Too factual A research paper is not merely a recitation, for instance, of the facts of Thomas Jefferson's life.

Too new Since you need print and nonprint sources and since the Internet alone is inadequate for research, a too new topic will have insufficient sources.

Too regional Localized topics generally lack sufficient resources to produce a well-developed paper.

Finally, one last bit of advice:

Choose a topic that you can word in a question, like these:

How did Jefferson affect American politics prior to his Presidency?

How do the Amish differ from the Mennonites?

What elements are necessary in a landfill design to protect future generations?

STEP 3: DO THE PRELIMINARY WORK

Before you get down to serious business, do some preliminary work. In the long run, it will save you hours, maybe even days. The preliminaries consist of three parts:

1. **Do some preliminary reading** to get background information about your topic. Check one or more of the following:

   A GENERAL ENCYCLOPEDIA, like

   > *The Encyclopedia Americana*
   > *Encyclopedia Britannica Micropaedia*

   A SPECIALIZED ENCYCLOPEDIA, like

   > *Encyclopedia of Social Sciences*
   > *Jewish Encyclopedia*
   > *Encyclopedia of World Literature in the 20th Century*

   OTHER GENERAL REFERENCES, like

   > *Internet*
   > *Current Biography*

After you have read, you will know whether or not your topic is sufficiently narrowed. Narrow further as necessary.

2. **Write a research question** that reflects the purpose of your paper, like these:

   How have Giacomo Torelli's stage ideas influenced modern theater?
   How does climate affect the migratory patterns of Canada geese?
   What characteristics distinguish ideogram pictographs from memory aids?

After you finish your research, you will answer the research question in the form of a thesis sentence. More on that later.

3. **Prepare a working outline.** The working outline guides your work, tells you in advance what specific information you need, and reminds you which materials

you should spend time reading and which are irrelevant to your work. It works for you, directs your research, helps you find your way toward an answer to your research question. Writing the working outline is a deductive thinking process. You have a general topic; it needs specific supporting details. What specific questions need answers to explain this big, general topic? Consider this example:

Research Question

What effects does laser technology have on general surgical procedures?

Specific Questions

1. Does laser technology speed surgery?
2. How do doctors decide when to use it?
3. Is the technology readily available?
4. What special facilities are necessary?
5. Are most doctors trained to do laser surgery?
6. Does it speed recovery?
7. Is it better for some surgeries than others?
8. Does it cost more than traditional surgery?
9. What dangers accompany laser surgery?
10. Do problems recur after laser surgery?
11. What damage can laser surgery cause?
12. Are there side effects from it?
13. What are the psychological problems before laser surgery?
14. Should the patient expect psychological effects afterward?
15. What effect does it have on the length of hospital stay?

Working Outline

From the list of questions, generate a working outline similar to this:

I. Elements for success
   A. Medical facilities (questions 3, 4, and 5)
   B. Patient condition (questions 1, 2, and 7)

II. Potential for problems (questions 9, 11, and 12)

III. Cost to patient
   A. Direct
      1. Surgery (question 8)
      2. Hospital stay (question 15)
   B. Indirect
      1. Recovery time (questions 6 and 10)
      2. Psychological impact (questions 13 and 14)

The working outline will ensure that you are considering the main aspects of the topic.

STEP 4: LOCATE SECONDARY RESOURCES

With your working outline in hand, you are ready to look for sources of information. You may use two kinds of resources:

Primary resources
> Materials that are contemporary to your subject—a book, an interview, a survey response, a letter, like John Audubon's diaries, paintings, and personal writings. Or Emily Dickinson's poetry and personal letters. (See Step 6)

Secondary resources
> Materials written later about someone or something, like books, magazine articles about

Audubon, his life, and his work. Or like Emily Dickinson's biography and books and articles about her and her poetry.

Depending on your purpose and your topic, secondary references may be sufficient.

Seek a wide variety of sources. A good researcher will use books, magazines, pamphlets, and newspapers as well as nonprint media such as audio, video, and electronic sources. For a paper of 1,500 to 2,000 words, plan to use a minimum of twenty to twenty-five resources, remembering that in the final analysis not every resource will be as valuable as it seems when you find it in the library.

Evaluate the sources. Before you haul home dozens of sources, check them for validity. Are they up-to-date sources from reliable authors and publishers? Have you found sources by those considered to be experts in the field you are researching? Did you skim possible sources for their usefulness by checking headings or chapter titles, the table of contents, and the index to evaluate the potential for your purpose and audience?

Check the following secondary resources for your topic:

General References

Consider general and specific encyclopedias, indexes, almanacs, dictionaries, and bibliographies.

Card or Computer Catalog

To find nonfiction books on an archival topic, use these tips:

- Look up headings broader than your topic.
- Look for other books by authors of sources already discovered.
- Use keyword searches.
- Read carefully and follow precisely computer catalog directions, usually found on an opening screen. Each system is slightly different, and each relies on different connecting words or symbols to make your search successful.

Periodical Indexes

For either print or electronic periodical indexes, use these tips:

- In order to find more information, look up headings broader than your narrowed topic.
- Follow through on "see also" and other cross-references.
- Use keyword searches.
- For best results with any electronic index, read carefully and follow precisely the directions, usually found on an opening screen.

Bibliographies

Check books or articles you have already discovered for lists of additional useful references. These often appear at the end of chapters and articles or at the back of books.

Indexes

Specialized indexes usually suggest valuable sources. Some of the most common ones include:

Education Index

General Science Index

Biological and Agricultural Index

Applied Science and Technology Index

Social Science Index

Humanities Index

Art Index

Book Review Digest

Print or Electronic

Newspaper Indexes Depending on the timeliness of your topic, you may find valuable information in current or archival newspaper indexes, including those on the Internet. (News Works indexes about 150 newspapers at <http://www.news works.com>.)

Non-book media Check the vertical file for pamphlets, government publications, and clippings. Check the audio-visual department for microforms, films, or other audio-visual references.

Other sources Always consider government agencies, associations, and museums, many of which have web sites with valuable information, or with links to other helpful sites.

Internet While the Internet is a viable source, check out these concerns:

Validity Anyone can put anything on the Internet. Thus, you must be able to determine the validity of anything you take from that source, including

Authorship

Author background

Date of publication (or most recent update)

Purpose of web site's sponsoring organization

Remember, if you cannot validate the information, do not use it for research.

Timing In general, turn to the Internet after you have exhausted other resources. Probably the best use of the Internet is for locating bibliographic information for other sources.

Finally, as you search for references, work smarter instead of harder. Think. Logic will tell you which kinds of references will likely offer the best—and the most—information.

STEP 5: PREPARE BIBLIOGRAPHY CARDS

When you have located adequate resources, prepare a bibliography card for each. Use a separate 3"x 5" card for each source. If you follow these guidelines, your Works Cited page will be a snap (see model paper, beginning on page 54.)

Author

- Begin the first line of the bibliography entry at the left margin of the card.
- Indent all subsequent lines five spaces.
- Begin with the author's name, written last name first followed by a comma and the first name and, if given, the middle initial.

Title

If the book or article is unsigned, begin with the title.

Titles must be written as follows:

- Underline or italicize titles of books and periodicals.
- Place quotation marks around the titles of articles.
- Capitalize words in titles correctly.
- Separate titles from subtitles with a colon.

Publishing Information

For books, include the following publishing information:

- List the place of publication.
- Follow the place of publication with a colon, a space, and the name of the publisher.
- Follow the name of the publisher with a comma and the date of publication.

For magazines, include the following publishing information:

- Follow magazine titles with the issue date.
- List dates in the correct manner, listing first the day of the month, then the month, and then the year.
- Follow the date with a colon, a space, and the page number.
- Omit commas between the month and the year.
- Abbreviate the names of months correctly.
- Where you need to name a state to identify the place of publication, use the two-letter abbreviation.

For Internet sources, include the following publishing information:

- Follow the title of the work with the date of publication or last update, if given.
- Follow the date with the full URL (Web site address), enclosed in angle brackets like this: <http://www.slu.edu/departments/english/research>.
- Finally, give the date of your visit, in parentheses.

Punctuation

In addition to punctuation detailed above, use periods correctly, as follows:

- Follow each item (author name, article title, book title, and publishing information) with a period.
- Use only one period when the author's middle initial is included.
- Omit the period after magazine titles.
- Omit the period after the Web site address.
- Use a period at the end of each bibliography entry.

Other Details

Include helpful information for yourself.

- If you used more than one library, list the name of the library where you found this source.
- For books, list the call number.
- Make a brief notation about important features for key references.

Above all, be consistent with all matters of style, using the same abbreviations, same format, same punctuation style, and same capitalization style throughout all your bibliography cards.

The following model bibliography cards should help you develop your own.

Greenberg, Jan. Advertising Courses:
How Advertising Works and the
People Who Make It Happen.
New York: Henry Holt and
Company, 1987.

includes separate section on international
advertising
borrowed from neighbor

McCommons, James. "The Comeback
of the Moose." Country Journal
May-June 1991: 28-32

good sidebar "Moose Facts"
school library

Blair, John. "Nuclear Energy Is Too
Costly, Dangerous to Be Effective."
The Evansville Courier 10 June
1991, Ind. ed.: A9.

local writer-may be good to interview

Barker, Joe. "Finding Information on the Internet: A Tutorial." 20 Sept. 1997. <http://www.lib.berkely.edu/ TeachingLib/Guides/Internet/ FindInfo.html> (14 Oct. 1997)

The following sample bibliography entries should help you use the correct form for a wide variety of situations.

Documentation
Forms

BOOKS

Book by a single author

> Benson, Jackson J. *The True Adventures of John Steinbeck, Writer*. New York: Penguin Books, 1984.

Book by two authors

> Gillgud, John, and John Miller. *Acting Shakespeare*. New York: Charles Scribner's Sons, 1991.

Book by three authors

> Hirsch, E. D., Jr., Joseph F. Kett, and James Trefil. *The Dictionary of Cultural Literacy: What Every American Needs to Know*. Boston: Houghton Mifflin Company, 1988.

Book with four or more authors

Shephard, Alan, Deke Slayton, Jay Barbree, and Howard Benedict. *Moon Shot: The Inside Story of America's Race to the Moon.* Atlanta: Turner Publishing, Inc., 1994.

Book with an editor or editors

Polking, Kirk, Joan Bloss, and Colleen Cannon, eds. *Writer's Encyclopedia.* Cincinnati: Writer's Digest Books, 1983.

Book by a corporate author

Luckman Interactive. *Best of the Web.* New York: Barnes and Noble Books, 1996.

Work in an anthology

Dove, Rita. "The Oriental Ballarina." *The Norton Anthology of African-American Literature.* Eds. Henry Louis Gates, Jr., and Nellie Y. McKay. New York: W. W. Norton & Company, 1997.

Multivolume or Translated work

Prost, Antoine, and Gerard Vincent, eds. *A History of Private Life.* Vol. 5. Trans. Arthur Goldhammer. Cambridge: Harvard University Press, 1991.

Edition of a book

Grauer, Robert T. and Gretchen Marx. *Essentials of the Internet.* 2nd ed. Upper Saddle River, NJ: Prentice Hall, 1997.

Government publications

United States. Dept. Of Labor. Bureau of Statistics. *Dictionary of Occupational Titles.* 6th ed. Washington: GPO, 1994.

Article in a reference book

"Steinbeck, John." *Contemporary Authors.* 1968.

Two notes about reference-book bibliography entries:

1. Many reference book articles, especially those in encyclopedias, are signed, the name appearing at the end of the article. Sometimes only initials appear. In that case, the initials will correspond to authors listed either in the front matter or in the index. When articles are signed, include the author's name in the bibliography entry.

2. No page number is necessary for alphabetically arranged references like dictionaries and encyclopedias.

Book without stated publication information

Use the following abbreviations when publication information is not included in the book:

n.p.	no place or publication given OR
	no publisher given
n.d.	no date of publication given
n. pag.	no pagination given

Insert the abbreviation in the bibliography entry at the point at which full information would otherwise appear.

MAGAZINES

Article from monthly periodical
LaRoe, Lisa Moore. "LaSalle's Last Voyage." *National Geographic* May 1997: 72-83.

Article from bimonthly periodical
Thwaites, Tim, et al. "Everything You Always Wanted to Know about Kangaroos." *International Wildlife* Sept.-Oct. 1997: 34-43.

Article from weekly or biweekly periodical
Plagens, Peter and Roy Sawhill. "Throw Out the Brushes: Commercial Artists Are Going Digital." *Newsweek* Sept. 1, 1997:75-77.

Unsigned article
"Active Traveler Directory." *Outside* July 1997: 149-157.

NEWSPAPERS

Signed article in daily paper
Varma, Kavita. "Footnotes in Electronic Age." *USA Today* 7 Feb. 1996, D7.

Unsigned article in quarterly paper
"Saving the Indiana Bat." *The Indiana Sierran* Winter 1997:4.

Letter to the editor
Carlson, Gavin C. Letter. *Princeton Post Dispatch* 8 Aug. 1997:10.

ELECTRONIC SOURCES
MATERIAL ON CD-ROM or DISKETTE

Unsigned article
"Computers in Education." *Facts on File News Digest.* CD-ROM. New York: Facts on File, Inc., 1998.

Signed article
Rosenberg, Victor. "Computers." *The New Grolier Electronic Encyclopedia.* CD-ROM. Danbury, CT: Grolier Electronic Publishing, Inc., 1996.

Signed newspaper article
Booth, William. "Rebuilding Wetlands: Nature Proves a Tough Act to Follow." *Washington [D.C.] Post* 30 Jan. 1990. Newsbank ENV 5:C13-14. CD-ROM. New Canaan, CT: Newsbank, Inc. 1993.

ON-LINE MATERIAL

On-line sources change rapidly in quantity, range, and accessibility. Thus the difficulty of documentation increases equally. Consider the following models as guides. For more information, you can find the most current on-line documentation forms—where else?—on-line.

Signed article with complete work
Kaplan, Lisa Faye. "Workplace: On Job Interview, Make Your First Few Seconds Count." *The Detroit News.* 28 Feb. 1997. <http://detnews.com/1997/accent/9702/28/02280028.htm> (22 Aug. 1997).

Signed article, no complete work
> Henahan, Sean. "Wetlands under Siege in Cities across Nation." 7 July 1997. <http://www.gene.om/ae/WN/SU/wet596.html> (3 Sept. 1997).

Unsigned article, no complete work
> "Defining Wetlands." 20 Feb. 1997. http://www.ceres.ca.gov/wetlands/introduction/defining_wetlands.html> (27 July 1997).

E-mail message
> Russ, Michael. <mkruss@evsc.k12.in.us> "Education URLs." 25 Aug. 1997. Personal e-mail. (25 Aug. 1997).

OTHER PRINT and NON PRINT RESOURCES

Pamphlet
> *On-line Scams: Potholes on the Information Highway.* Washington, D.C.: FTC Bureau of Consumer Protection, Office of Consumer and Business Education, Mar. 1996.

Radio or Television Program
> *Latest Edition.* Writ. Laura Lexter. PBS. WJXT, Princeton, 18 Sept. 1997.

Letter
> Roth, Sally. Letter to the author. 29 Oct. 1997.

Map or chart
> *Canada.* Map. Chicago: Rand McNally, 1998.

Lecture, speech, or address
> Kochesky, Leonard. Address. Concurrent Sess. Midwest Birding Association Conference. Cleveland, OH, 29 Sept. 1997.

Survey or experiment
> Conrad, LaTisha. "Survey of Backpackers' Attitudes toward Weather Warnings." Colton, Ariz., 14-29 May, 1997.

Film or Videocassette
> *It's a Wonderful Life.* Dir. Frank Capra. Perf. James Stewart, Donna Reed, Lionel Barrymore, and Thomas Mitchell. 1946. Videocassette. Republic, 1988.

STEP 6: USE PRIMARY RESOURCES

Read your secondary references thoroughly enough to know which primary sources will be of benefit and how they can enhance your research paper. Then, considering your narrowed topic, purpose, and audience, think about the most likely possibilities for primary sources: interviews, surveys, experiments, and/or letters.

Interviews

Make an honest effort to seek available community resources. They will enrich your research. After locating a potential source for an interview, follow logical steps for the interview process.

- Arrange for an appointment.
- Prepare a list of questions to address your purpose and specific topic.

- Write a letter or e-mail confirmation and include a list of questions for the interview.
- Prioritize your questions.
- Conduct the interview in a timely, gracious fashion.
- Listen critically to the interviewee's responses and ask logical follow-up questions.
- Express appreciation both at the conclusion of the interview and in a follow-up letter.

Surveys

If your purpose and topic suggest the need for it, plan and conduct a survey. Use these steps:

- Include questions seeking information directly related to your purpose and topic.
- Word the questions objectively.
- If necessary, provide for a way to identify the source of responses.
- Conduct the survey in a timely, gracious fashion.
- Tabulate the results fairly.

Experiments

If your purpose and topic suggest the need for it, plan and conduct an experiment. Follow these steps:

- Develop a clear hypothesis.
- Design testing procedures that will prove or disprove the hypothesis.
- Gather accurate data and analyze it impartially.
- Reach a logical conclusion based on the data.

Letters

If your purpose and topic suggest it, write effective letters or e-mail to potential sources. Follow these guidelines:

- Ask for specific information relevant to your research question.
- Allow ample response time.
- Express appreciation to those who respond.

Finally, no matter which primary resources you choose to use, manage your time well.

STEP 7: TAKE NOTES

The following directives apply to note taking from print and nonprint sources, from electronic media or multimedia.

General Guidelines

Before you begin taking notes, number your bibliography cards. You will use this number to code your note cards to indicate the source from which they come.

- Use a separate note card (3" x 5" or 6" x 10") for each idea, even if you write only a few words on a card.
- Write in ink, only on one side of the card.
- While you may develop your own form of shorthand, use only abbreviations which will make sense to you later.
- On every note card, in the upper right corner, write the number, circled, to identify its source.

- Follow the source number with a hyphen and then the page number(s).
- On the top line of every note card add a slug—a title that identifies the topic of the note and correspond to a heading or subheading in your preliminary outline.

As you work, strive for accuracy and completeness. Consider these reminders about note taking:

Plagiarism

Avoid plagiarism. Plagiarism is literary theft, using someone else's words or ideas as if they were your own. It's a serious offense, usually with serious penalties attached—like automatic failure for the paper or even the course. To learn how to avoid plagiarism, study the following passages:

Original Passage

The cost-effective production of white corn is important to anyone who likes cereal for breakfast, tacos for lunch, tortillas for dinner, or fritos for a snack. But reducing operating costs in order to keep down consumer costs is an ongoing problem for farmers. As we walked through the grain-bin area, Mr. Z. pointed to a 3,500-gallon propane tank. During harvest, he explained, the tank was filled every other day. Then, to reduce costs, Mr. Z. spent $70,000 to design and build a cob burner that gasifies the corncobs and turns them into fuel. The operation has cut the fuel bill by about 60%. Now the propane fuel tank is filled only once a week.

Plagiarized (Not Acceptable)

Reducing the operating costs of white corn production is an ongoing problem, but one farmer has reduced costs by spending $70,000 to design and build a cob burner that gasifies the corncobs and turns them into fuel.

Reworded, Partly Quoted, and Documented (Acceptable)

Farmers struggle to reduce the cost of producing white corn, a staple for many Americans who like cereal and tortillas. One farmer has cut his fuel consumption in half by using what had once been thrown away: the corncobs. As Mr. Z. explained, the $70,000 cob burner "gasifies the corncobs and turns them into fuel" (Kamp 16).

(Note that exact words appear in quotation marks and, along with the reworded portions, are acknowledged by documentation at the end of the paragraph.)

Reworded and Documented (Acceptable)

Representative of farmers' creative approaches to cut the cost of producing white corn, one farmer has given the term "recycling" a new twist. For $70,000 he designed and built a cob burner that turns corncobs to gas that can in turn be used for fuel. He has eliminated the pile of cobs that accumulated out back and at the same time cut his fuel consumption by more than half (Kamp16).

(Note this completely reworded passage omits exact words. Since it is a paraphrase, however, credit must be given to the source.)

Avoid plagiarism by following three rules:

> **DO NOT** use exact words from a source without putting them inside quotation marks and giving credit to the source.

> **DO NOT** reword a passage without giving credit to the source.

> **DO NOT** summarize a passage without giving credit to the source.

Kinds of Notes

Not all note cards are alike. In fact, you will want to take advantage of a variety of different kinds of notes as they best suit your purpose.

Direct quotation notes use the source's exact words, exact spelling, exact punctuation. If a word is misspelled or incorrectly used, add the word *sic* in brackets, meaning "thus," to clarify that the error is not yours.

Remember to avoid excessive quotations, using them for fewer than 20% of your notes.

Use direct quotations only under these conditions:

- When an authority's words carry weight.
- When the quotation is concise and powerful.
- When it would be impossible to restate as effectively in your own words.

Use quotation marks every time you use an author's exact words; otherwise, you will fall into the error of plagiarism.

Destruction

(16) 45

"Thanks to a double-dealing USDA, Swampbuster's a bust, wetlands are being destroyed, and taxpayers are getting soaked for it."

Partial quotation notes are mostly summaries in your own words, quoting only some key phrase. These notes follow a few simple rules:

Use the ellipsis (a series of three periods separated by a space between each, like this . . .) to represent the omission of a word or words. If the omission occurs at the end of a sentence, a fourth period serves as the end mark.

Use brackets [like this] to insert your own words inside a quotation or to change a word form (for example, from usual to usual[ly]). Never use parentheses for brackets.

Always remember to use quotation marks around the quoted material.

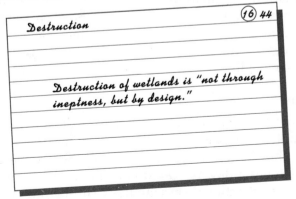

Destruction

(16) 44

Destruction of wetlands is "not through ineptness, but by design."

Précis notes summarize in about one-third the length of the original. To be accurate, a précis must maintain the same tone and the same message as the original. Study the following example:

Original Passage

The food habits of birds make them especially valuable to agriculture. Because birds have higher body temperatures, more rapid digestion, and greater energy than most other animals, they require more food. Nestling birds grow very rapidly, requiring huge amounts of food. They usually consume as much or more than their own weight in soft-bodied insects every day.

For instance, robins have been observed to gain eight times their original weight the first eight days of their lives. Insect-eating birds must fill their stomachs five to six times daily because they digest their food so fast and because of the large amount of indigestible material in insects. One young robin, weighing three ounces, consumed 165 cutworms weighing 5 1/2 ounces in one day. If a ten-pound baby ate at the same rate, he or she would eat 18 1/3 pounds of food in a day.

Of course, birds cannot control insects completely, but they are of great value. By using soil- and water-conserving practices, farmers and ranchers could probably double the population of helpful birds. Field and farmstead windbreaks, living fences, shrub buffers, grass waterways, and farm ponds are only a few of the many land use practices useful in attracting and increasing beneficial forms of wildlife.

Précis

A bird's metabolism causes it to eat relatively more than most other animals. In addition, since insects aren't fully digestible, insect-eating birds may fill their stomachs five or six times a day. We can double the numbers of insect-eaters by attracting them with trees, shrubs, and ponds.

Outline notes may appear in formal outline style or look more like a list. In either case, it is particularly appropriate when noting a series of points or steps.

Kinds of Wetlands
5 Kinds   (28) 21
Coastal

1) Marine (salt water)
2) estuarine (where salt meets fresh)
Freshwater
90% { *3) lacustrine (lakes)*
4) riverine (along rivers, streams)
5) palustrine (marshes, swamps, bogs)

Paraphrased notes are a rewording of the original in about the same number of words; thus, they are most likely to lean toward plagiarism. Nevertheless, the paraphrased note is essential in two situations: when you need to simplify complicated text or when you need to clarify a passage. Study these passages:

Original Passage

Windows are the home's giant energy eaters. As the world grows more energy conscious, homeowners seek more ways to seal the leaks that allow heating dollars to flow freely through escape routes. They add insulation to the ceiling; they add weather stripping around doors and windows; they caulk cracks and crevices; they add storm windows or thermal panes. After all such measures have been taken, however, there seems little else to do. Wrong! About 35% of household heat can escape through windows—even those carefully caulked and protected with storm windows.

Paraphrase

Homeowners who are concerned about energy do everything they know to conserve. They add ceiling insulation, weather stripping, caulking, and storm windows, hoping to stop the exodus of heat from their homes and dollars from their thinning wallets. Unfortunately, most of those homeowners, believing they have done all they can to conserve heat, ignore the expanse of glass called windows. About 35% of heat loss occurs here. In fact, windows remain the worst enemy to effective energy conservation.

Combination notes combine any of the other types. They are probably the most useful and the most used.

(1) Combines
   outline
   and text

Farmer's Destruction of Wetlands   (14)   19

Remove incentives to farmers to eliminate wetlands:

1) 1986 Tax Reform Act (can't deduct)
2) 1985 Swampbuster "removes federal flood and crop insurance and price supports" if destroyed
3) 1982 Coastal Barrier Resources Act

(2) Combines list with
writer's response

(20) 32–33

> Urban Wetlands
> 4,000 acres – Portland, OR
> 1,232 acres – Ft. Collins, CO
> 13,000 acres – within Brooklyn
> and Queens
> 6 sq. mi. – Madison, WI
> 108 acres – Bellevue, WA
> Find out:
> How many acres in 6 sq. mi.

(3) Combines
quotation
and
summary
statement
explaining
significance
of quotation

> Laws protecting
>
> (14)   19
>
> Section 404 "exempts activities connected
> with 'normal' farming and forestry
> practices. . ."
>
> (Here is where biggest
> conversions occur.)

General Warnings

Finally, be alert to the following general warnings about
note taking:

- Avoid taking too many notes from only one or
  two sources.
- Use relevant, timely sources suitable for your
  topic.
- Take only notes that correspond to your working
  outline or to your revised working outline.
- Revise your working outline as your reading and
  note taking suggest.

STEP 8: WRITE THE FINAL OUTLINE

You have revised your working outline as you have taken notes, found additional information, or the lack of it. Now you need to make a final revision. Use these guidelines:

Write a thesis sentence. Your thesis sentence answers your research question (see Step 3, part 2). Your outline must reflect your thesis. In other words, the sum of the parts of your outline must equal the thesis statement.

A thesis

- answers your research question
- is a single declarative sentence with one main clause
- states your position or findings on the topic
- states the specific focus the paper will have
- suggests what the conclusion will say
- reflects what your notes provide

A thesis is **NOT**

- a question
- a statement beginning "The purpose of this paper is . . ."
- a statement of the topic
- made of multiple main clauses

Examples:

When wetlands are destroyed, the reduction of the water table affects life of all kinds, even that of the average city dweller.

While Steinbeck's depiction of the Great Depression in *The Grapes of Wrath* bears historical accuracy, at least one family showed little similarity between its life and that of the Joads.

Government, private organizations, and individuals are all working to solve what seems to be the insurmountable problem of homelessness.

Robotics of low, medium, and high technology have revolutionized industry by making it less dependent on but also safer for humans.

Sort your note cards using the following plan:

- Sort the note cards according to their slugs—those topics which came from your working outline.

- Check your note cards for slugs not on your outline and then decide if you need to add a heading or subheading or if you simply have irrelevant information.

- Check outline topics for which you have no note cards and then decide if you need to change your outline or return to the library for more information.

Choose an organization pattern that will best reflect your purpose and topic:

1. chronological order
2. spatial order
3. order of importance
   - from most important to least important (best for newspaper articles which the reader may not finish)
   - from second most important to least important to most important (best for persuasive papers assuming a skeptical reader)

- from least important to most important (commonly used for general work, including research papers)

Check the structure of your outline. It should follow these guidelines:

Your outline must illustrate that you have divided the topic into relatively equal parts.

- To have six subheadings under A and none under B suggests illogical division.
- To have eight subheadings under II and two under III suggests illogical division.

Avoid the illogical use of a subheading designated *A* without designated *B* or a *1* without a *2*.

- Use headings and subheadings which are mutually exclusive. For instance, to categorize college students as *male*, *female*, and *older* is illogical.
- To categorize them instead as *traditional* and *nontraditional* with *male* and *female* as subheadings under each is logical.

Use logical divisions, divided by a single criterion.

- For instance, to divide pies into *homemade*, *fruit*, *best restaurant*, and *recipes* is illogical.
- Division by a single criterion, where pies are made, for example, is logical: *homemade*, *restaurant purchased*, or *bakery purchased*.

Avoid fifth- and sixth-level divisions for which you have nothing more than a sentence to write.

Maintain parallel structure. All topics within a level must be parallel to each other.

Follow the conventions for punctuation, indentation, and capitalization.

- Roman numerals must be arranged so that the periods align.
- Each letter in second-level divisions is capitalized and followed by a period.
- Arabic numbers in third-level divisions are followed by periods.
- The first word in headings and subheadings begins with an uppercase letter, and the other words (except proper nouns and adjectives) begin with lowercase letters.
- Omit periods after headings and subheadings.

Study a model. The following is the outline for the model paper beginning on page 54.

THESIS STATEMENT: When earth's citizens recognize wetlands' values, perhaps they will be more concerned about the protection of those vanishing areas.

I. Definition of wetlands
    A. Definition by category
    B. Definition by characteristics
    C. Definition by law

II. Destruction of wetlands
    A. Losses
        1. Past
        2. Continuing
    B. Causes

III. Effects of destruction
   A. On plant life
   B. On animal life
      1. Marine creatures
      2. Waterfowl
      3. Other wildlife
   C. On water
      1. Storage area
      2. Filtering system
      3. Storm protection
   D. On biosphere

IV. Value to humans
   A. Economic impact
   B. Economic controversy
   C. Resulting efforts

Analyze the Model Outline

The four main headings, when added together, equal the thesis statement.

$$I + II + III + IV = \text{Thesis}$$

A heading with its subheadings is the equivalent of a paragraph with its supporting details.

$$II = A + B$$

$$A = 1 + 2$$

- The outline demonstrates relatively equal subheadings.
- Note how in each category the subheadings, taken together, equal their main headings.

- The outline moves from the general to the specific.
- It is arranged by order of importance, from definition to effects to value, building toward reader understanding.

Remember that the outline maps out the body of the paper. It will be your paragraph-by-paragraph guide for writing the draft.

STEP 9: WRITE THE DRAFT

Use the following general suggestions as you write the first draft of your paper.

General Suggestions

If you write with pen and paper, write on every other line and only on one side of your paper. However, if you write at the computer, set the format command for double spacing. Make sure to save everything—even apparently irrelevant note cards and early drafts.

Write the Introduction

Make a conscious effort in your introduction to attract reader interest. Use one of the following techniques for an effective introduction:

- Startle the reader with facts or statistics.
- Describe a compelling condition or situation.
- Use a story or conversation to introduce an event.
- Explain a conflict or inconsistency.
- Ask a provocative question.

- Use a quotation, adage, or proverb.
- State or imply your thesis statement in the introduction.

Use temporary documentation as you write the body paragraphs, and be sure to list the source and page number for all information.

- Use a kind of shorthand from your note cards: the source number and the page number from the upper right corner.
- For instance, 3-17 is a shorthand temporary documentation for page 17 from the bibliography card marked number 3.

Be sure to enclose the exact words of a source in quotation marks.

- Before you finish with a note card, double check for quotation marks.
- Their careless omission can cause you to be accused of plagiarism.

Document anything that comes from either a primary or secondary resource:

- quotations or partial quotations
- others' ideas, even if in your words
- others' opinions, even if in your words
- little-known facts, even if easily proven

Do **not** document

- personal opinions and interpretations
- well-known facts

If in doubt, document. Better safe than sorry.

Write the Body Paragraphs

Use the following general guidelines for writing effective body paragraphs:

- Make your paragraphs correspond to your outline or your revised outline.
- Follow the organization established in your outline or your revised outline.
- Include in each paragraph a stated or implied topic sentence.
- Use your note cards to develop support for each paragraph.
- Maintain unity.
- Blend material from your note cards into your own sentences.
- Blend quoted material into your own sentences.
- Use tables and figures that stand alone, but your text must be clear without the tables or figures. Blend references to tables and figures into your text.
- Use transitional words, phrases, sentences, and paragraphs to connect ideas within and between paragraphs.
- Omit irrelevant material from note cards that really do not support any of your main ideas.

Study a Model Paragraph and Note Cards

The following illustrate how note cards become the text of your paper. Notice, too, the temporary documentation.

Water Storage

(10) 2

Wetlands are "'hydrologic modifiers'— storage places for water." They store water during rainy seasons and then let it seep out slowly. Stops severe droughts and floods.

Water Storage

(26) 4

"Buildings, concrete and asphalt waterproof" big areas so causes run-off.

Water Storage

(26) 7

Re: 1-acre swap, 1-foot deep holds 330,000 gallons water "Thus whenever a swap is filled or drained, another large quantity of water is lost from the underground water supply and made to run off more quickly to aggravate flooding downstream."

Paragraph

Wetlands, however, do more than protect living plants and animals. They also work as so-called "hydrologic modifiers," storing water and then releasing it slowly, reducing the impact of floods and droughts (10-2). Because giant parking lots, acres of buildings, masses of concrete, and many square miles of pavement literally waterproof the land, rain water cannot soak in; so it is concentrated in large runoffs. Floods result. On the other hand, a one-acre swamp filled with a foot of water holds 330,000 gallons. "Thus whenever a swamp is filled or drained, another large quantity of water is lost from the underground water supply and made to run off more quickly to aggravate flooding problems downstream" (26-4, 7). As wetlands biologist Keith Poole explained in a personal interview, "We all live downstream."

Poole
(interview)

Water Storage

"We all live downstream."

(Referring to floods and pollution)

Conclude your Paper Effectively

Use one or more of the following techniques to effectively conclude your paper.

- Provide a summary.
- Reach a conclusion.
- Make an observation.
- Issue a challenge.
- Refer to the introduction.

Once you finish a draft of your paper, set it aside for later revision. Meanwhile, however, you may want to ask a peer editor to read your draft and suggest ways you might improve upon each of the guidelines above.

STEP 10: REVISE THE DRAFT

After you put distance between you and your paper, you are ready to revise. Use these questions to check for areas needing revision.

Revision Checklist

1. Do I do in my paper what the thesis statement says I will, i.e., answer the research question?
2. Do I have a defensible reason for arranging paragraphs in the order I do?
3. Did I follow my outline or its revision?
4. Have I maintained the same attitude throughout my paper?
5. Are all of my paragraphs well written?
   a. Does each have a topic sentence, stated or implied?

    b. Does each include enough supporting details to defend its topic?

    c. Does each paragraph maintain unity, i.e., does every detail included support the topic sentence?

    d. Do transitional words, phrases, or sentences connect ideas within paragraphs?

    e. Does each paragraph have a concluding idea or sentence (where needed)?

6. Do transitional words, phrases, or sentences connect ideas between paragraphs?

7. When I combine the topic sentences from each of the paragraphs, do they logically equal the thesis statement?

8. Have I written grammatically sound sentences, avoiding fragments, run-ons, comma splices, dangling and misplaced modifiers, and redundancies?

9. Have I used parallel structures for coordinating elements?

10. Have I varied my sentences by length?

11. Have I varied my sentences by structure?

12. Do my sentences create emphasis for important points?

13. Did I check for accurate word choice?

14. Did I check the grammar, mechanics, and usage?

STEP 11: PREPARE THE FINAL MANUSCRIPT

As you prepare the final manuscript, follow these guidelines for general manuscript form, first page formatting, documentation, and the Works Cited page.

General Manuscript Form

See the model beginning on page 54 which illustrates the following manuscript form.

- Use good quality 8 1/2″ x 11″ white paper, printed on only one side.
- Double space the entire paper, including long quotations and the Works Cited page.
- Maintain a one-inch margin on all four sides of all pages.
- Maintain a running head made up of your last name and the page number one-half inch from the top of each page, with page numbers flush with the right margin.
- Indent five spaces for each paragraph.
- Avoid having a single line of a paragraph appear at the bottom or top of a page.
- If you have tables or figures, put them as close as possible to the text they support or illustrate.
- If you quote poetry, quote up to three poetic lines by using quotation marks around the quoted work and separating the lines of poetry with the slash (/) mark. If you quote more than three lines, treat the poetry as a long quotation (see Documentation below) and maintain the poetic form.

Formatting the First Page

Research papers generally do not require a title page (If yours does, see below.) Thus, on the first page of your text at the left margin, enter the following identifying details one inch from the top, on four double-spaced lines:

- your name
- your teacher's name
- course title
- due date

Double space after the due date and enter the title, centered on the page. Use only initial uppercase letters but use initial lowercase letters for prepositions, articles, and coordinating conjunctions. Do not use quotation marks or underscore or italics.

If your paper requires a title page, include three kinds of information, balanced left to right and top to bottom: title, author, and course identification.

If your paper requires an outline page, use correct format (see a model, pages 37–38) and number the pages with lowercase Roman numerals.

Documentation

Include documentation after every quotation, précis, or paraphrase.

Place parenthetical documentation in the sentence where a pause would naturally occur: at the end of a sentence, at the end of a clause, at the end of a phrase.

After any quotation, précis, or paraphrase, enter a space (as between words). Then in parentheses, write the source name and the page number.

Use the author's last name to indicate the source:

Example:
The stream waters flowing out of such wetlands are "cleaner than most municipally treated water" (Klockenbrink 72) and teem with fish, plants, and birds.

If there are two authors, use both last names.

Example:
Annual wetlands productivity in Georgia's Alcovy River Swamp equals roughly a $3.1 million impact (Goodwin and Niering 4-7).

If there is no author, use the title, shortened if possible. Use quotation marks or underscore as appropriate for the title.

Example:
Earlier labeled "the Rodney Dangerfield of the environment" ("Importance" 2), wetlands are gaining respect as an integral part of life's interdependence.

If you use more than one work by a given author, identify both the author and the work. Separate the author's name from the title with a comma.

Example:
"Since 1950 over 4.5 million acres of wetlands have been lost in the Mississippi flyway alone" (Kusler, "Roles" 43).

Use no punctuation between the name of the source and the page number.

Place sentence-end punctuation immediately *after* the close parenthesis.

Place close quotation marks *before* the open parenthesis.

If the author's name appears in the text of the paper, place only the page number in parentheses.

Example:
> In an editorial, Peter A. A. Berle wrote, "Economists still are not good at comparing the value of a wetlands ecosystem with that of a shopping-center parking lot. . ." (6).

If the quotation ends with an ellipsis, insert the parenthetical documentation after the close of the quotation marks but before the final period. See example immediately above.

If you use indirect information, acknowledge the secondary source in the documentation. If possible, use the original source for authenticity.

Example:
> As Chief Seattle said in 1854, "Whatever happens to the beasts soon happens to man" (qtd. in Walter 40).

If a summary comes from several sources, all sources appear in a single parenthetical reference. Separate listed sources by semicolons.

Example:
> Farmers, environmentalists, and government agree that agriculture is to blame for 87% of recent wetland losses (Walter 28; "Saving Swamps" 44; Tiner 32).

In citing classic literary works, which are available in many editions, instead of citing page numbers, cite chapters, acts and scenes, lines, parts, cantos, etc.

Example:

In *Hamlet*, the reference "to thine own self be true" (1.3.82) may be one approach to self love.

Works Cited Page

Use the following guidelines to format your Works Cited page:

- Continue the running head on the Works Cited page.
- Center the title "Works Cited" one inch from the top of the page. Do not use quotation marks, underscore, or italics. Use initial uppercase letters.
- Double-space the entire page, both within and between entries.
- Begin the first entry one double space below the title.
- Begin all entries at the left margin, but subsequent lines are indented five spaces.
- Adhere to the format for bibliography cards. (See pages 17-23.)
- Enter all sources in alphabetical order by the first word on your bibliography card: author's last name or title of article. If a title begins with *A, An,* or *The,* alphabetize by the next word.
- Be sure every parenthetical citation included in your text has a corresponding entry on the Works Cited page.

If you cite two or more sources by the same author, follow these rules:

- Give author's name in only the first entry.

- Subsequent entries indicate the same author by beginning with three hyphens followed by a period.
- Arrange all the publications in alphabetical order by title.

Example:

> Steinhart, Peter. "No Net Loss." *Audubon* July 1990: 18-21.
> ---. "Standing Room Only." *National Wildlife* April-May 1989: 46+.

- Maintain a one-inch bottom margin.
- Continue entries on additional pages as necessary, omitting the "Works Cited" title on further pages and beginning the text one inch from the top.

Finally, remember to make a copy of your paper.

STEP 12: PROOFREAD THE PAPER

Proofreading is an exacting task. Allow ample time for final checking, following these guidelines:

Proofreading Checklist

- Look carefully at every word, checking for keyboarding errors or misspellings.
- Avoid dividing words at the ends of lines.
- Check for accurate punctuation.
- Check for grammatical errors, especially errors that you know you have made in the past.
- Check for consistent point of view, most likely third-person point of view.

- Use consistent verb tenses.
- Use correct manuscript style throughout the text.
- Check the Works Cited page for accuracy:

    Are the title and running head accurate?

    Are names spelled correctly?

    Have you capitalized accurately?

    Are punctuation marks correct, especially in relationship to other punctuation?

    Does each entry end with a period?

    Have you underlined and used quotation marks accurately?

    Is the list of entries correctly alphabetized?

    Have you correctly cited multiple works by the same author?

- Check direct quotations to make sure they are accurate.
- Check your text against your note cards to make sure you used necessary quotation marks, thus avoiding plagiarism.
- Check for accurate documentation, including correctly spelled names and correct page numbers.
- Check that every source cited in your paper is also listed on the Works Cited page.
- Check that only sources cited in your paper are included on the Works Cited page.
- Make sure your paper reflects your best effort.

Analyze a
Complete Model

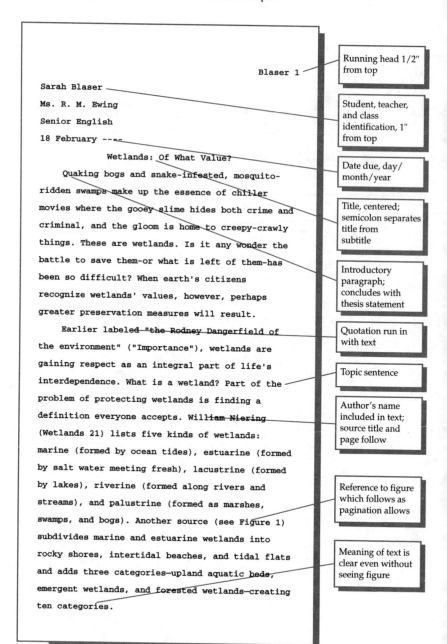

Blaser 1

Sarah Blaser

Ms. R. M. Ewing

Senior English

18 February ----

Wetlands: Of What Value?

Quaking bogs and snake-infested, mosquito-
ridden swamps make up the essence of chiller
movies where the gooey slime hides both crime and
criminal, and the gloom is home to creepy-crawly
things. These are wetlands. Is it any wonder the
battle to save them-or what is left of them-has
been so difficult? When earth's citizens
recognize wetlands' values, however, perhaps
greater preservation measures will result.

Earlier labeled "the Rodney Dangerfield of
the environment" ("Importance"), wetlands are
gaining respect as an integral part of life's
interdependence. What is a wetland? Part of the
problem of protecting wetlands is finding a
definition everyone accepts. William Niering
(Wetlands 21) lists five kinds of wetlands:
marine (formed by ocean tides), estuarine (formed
by salt water meeting fresh), lacustrine (formed
by lakes), riverine (formed along rivers and
streams), and palustrine (formed as marshes,
swamps, and bogs). Another source (see Figure 1)
subdivides marine and estuarine wetlands into
rocky shores, intertidal beaches, and tidal flats
and adds three categories-upland aquatic beds,
emergent wetlands, and forested wetlands-creating
ten categories.

Running head 1/2"
from top

Student, teacher,
and class
identification, 1"
from top

Date due, day/
month/year

Title, centered;
semicolon separates
title from
subtitle

Introductory
paragraph;
concludes with
thesis statement

Quotation run in
with text

Topic sentence

Author's name
included in text;
source title and
page follow

Reference to figure
which follows as
pagination allows

Meaning of text is
clear even without
seeing figure

Blaser 2

The terms categorizing wetlands, however,
still do not completely define them. As one
writer explains the problem,

> There is no generic swamp. Rather there are
> acid swamps, cedar swamps, river swamps, bay
> swamps, blackgum swamps, and cypress swamps.
> There are fens in Massachusetts, bogs in
> Maine, prairie potholes in the Dakotas and
> sea grass beds and mangrove forests in
> Florida (Booth 13).

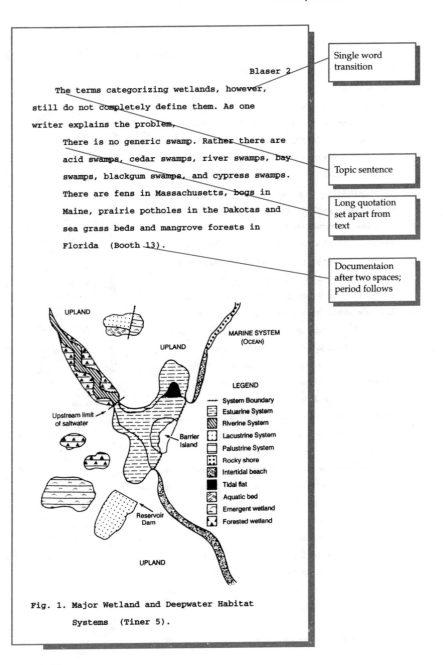

Fig. 1. Major Wetland and Deepwater Habitat
Systems (Tiner 5).

Blaser 3

To further complicate the problem of clear
definition, wetlands change, becoming marshes,
wet meadows, eventually perhaps shrub-or tree-
filled swamps (Niering, "Swamp" 8). In addition,
size does not define a wetland. In fact, the most
threatened wetlands are not the big or famous or
maybe not even the obvious, but instead,
"scattered tracts of private property you might
drive right past" (Easterbook 40).

The Supreme Court, however, has finally
handed down the legal definition. Wetlands are
areas "inundated or saturated by surface or
ground water at a frequency and duration
sufficient to support, and that under normal
circumstances do support, a prevalence of
vegetation tyically adapted for life in saturated
soil conditions" ("Defining Wetlands"). To put it
plainly, if the soil is wet enough often enough
to affect the vegetation, the area is a wetland.

Depending on how one defines wetlands and
depending on whose statistics one reads, anywhere
from half to two-thirds the United States'
wetlands have been destroyed.

Environmentalist Malcolm F. Baldwin said in
1987 that only 99 million acres remained, an area
about the size of California. That, he said, is
"less than one-half of 215 million acres " (17)
of original wetlands. Examining only the lower 48
states, a Connecticut College team estimated in
1975 that wetlands had diminished from 127
million acres to 70 million acres, only 3.5% of
the total land (Goodwin and Niering 3).

Transition

Second source by
Niering

Transition

Transition

Quotation woven
into writer's own
sentence

Quotation for
authenticity

Paraphrase of
previous quotation
for clarity

Date included;
timeliness
important to topic

Words and
numbers for large
numbers

Figures for
numbers over ten

Shows
disagreement with
above figures,
which helps
support idea that
wetlands are hard
to define

Co-authors

Most authorities agree that the United States is
losing 400,000 to 500,000 acres of wetlands a year.
Some specific areas, however, seem to have suffered
more than others. For instance, along the lower
Mississippi Valley, only 20% of the wetlands once
covered with hardwood forest remains, and an
additional 100,000 acres disappear every year. In
that area alone in just 35 years, over 4.5 million
acres of wetlands have disappeared (Kusler, "Roles"
43).

The grievous losses are attributed to a number
of factors. A 1983 Environmental Law Institute
publication names seven categories of wetlands
losses:

1. Drainage (for crop and timber production
   and mosquito control)
2. Dredging and channelization (for navigation,
   flood protection, housing developments, and
   irrigation)
3. Dikes, dams (for flood control, irrigation,
   storm surge protection)
4. Filling (for building roads, bridges,
   developments; for utility lines and solid
   waste disposal)
5. Discharges into water (like herbicides,
   sewage, materials from dredging and land
   development)
6. Water pumping (for municipal water supplies
   and irrigation)
7. Mining (for sand, gravel, coal, peat)
   (Kusler, Heritage 8-9)

In the United States, however, farmers,
environmentalists, and the government agree
that agriculture is to blame for 87% of

Cites general agreement

Publisher named for credibility

Colon to introduce formal list

Summarizes two pages from sources; enumerates causes

Blaser 5

recent wetland losses (Walter 28; "Saving Swamps" 44; Tiner 32).

→ *Three sources supporting same opinion*

Given these vast losses, the real question is why should anyone care? As one old sage put it, "Marshes are more than muskrats and mosquitoes" (qtd. In Sporre 23). At the same time, however, "something lurks in mire and mud that frightens us" (Steinhart, "No Loss" 20). The general public, accordingly, has been slow to realize the importance of wetlands. Peter Steinhart laments in his essay, "As wetlands vanish, we begin to see their value. Research shows them to be the most productive landscapes in nature" ("No Loss" 18). What happens, then, as the wetlands are destroyed? These swamps and bogs maintain a unique environment that supports countless species of both plants and animals, making them a "vast genetic resource" ("Saving Swamps" 45). Consequently, to destroy wetlands is to destroy a resource for plants and animals from the bottom of the food chain all the way up to humans.

→ *Transitional paragraph; moves from causes to effects*

→ *Shows source not original*

→ *Present tense*

→ *Unsigned article*

→ *Introduces next point; begins discussion of effects*

→ *Colon introduces list*

Exploring the destruction of that resource leads first to the wide variety of plant life supported by wetlands: cattails, water hyacinths, reeds, rushes, shrubs, bushes, and, surprisingly, trees. In fact, many wetlands originally supported massive timber growth. While the loss of that harvested timber is easily identified, the loss of other plant life will not be so obvious. For instance, probably the most unusual wetlands plants are the small, inconspicuous carnivores. A University of North Carolina botanist warns, "Unless we take prompt action to preserve the native habitats, carnivorous plants will vanish

→ *Transitional phrase*

→ *Transitional clause*

→ *Identifies occupation to establish authority*

Blaser 6

in a few short years " (Bender 74). Carnivorous
plants, like every other form of life on this
planet, play a role in the overall ecological
scheme. Their destruction ultimately affects
the balance of nature.

    The effect of wetlands destruction on plant
life tells only half the story. The other half
belongs to animal life, beginning with marine
creatures. Of all of the fish and shellfish
brought in commercially and privately from both
east and west coasts, between one-half and
two-thirds of the species "rely on coastal wetlands
for food, spawning, and/or nursery areas"
(Williamson 42). To destroy those wetlands,
therefore, is to take seafood off restaurant
menus and grocery shelves.

    The situation is just as serious for waterfowl.
"In the cycle of a duck's life, wetlands are the
one ingredient that cannot be altered without
causing almost irreversible damage to the duck
population as a whole "("Wetlands Ducks" 63).
Sadly, the evidence is already at hand. After the
destruction of 90% of the 94,000 acres of wetlands
in Nebraska's Rainwater basin, migrating waterfowl
were so crowded that 80,000 birds died there of
avian cholera in 1980 (Baldwin 27). While research
focuses on waterfowl (because hunting licenses help
finance the research), hundreds of thousands of
other birds are affected in similar ways.
In short, three-quarters of all of the birds found
in North America "depend upon wetlands for resting,
feeding, or nesting "(Steinhart,"No Loss" 18).

Transitional
sentence

Partial quotation
run into text

Parallel infinitive
phrases for clear
cause-effect
relationship

Topic sentence
with transitional
phrase; continues
discussion of effects

Parenthetical
explanation

Quotation that
concludes
paragraph's topic

Blaser 7

In terms of wildlife in general, Gregg
Easterbrook points out that while the public pays
attention to endangered species like pandas and
grizzlies, they ignore the "germline," a word he
coined to refer to "the general genetic heritage,
especially of lesser organisms that form the
majority" (41) of other organisms. The germline,
most likely found in swamps, should concern earth
citizens even more than the individual species. As
Chief Seattle said in 1854, "What is man without
the beasts? If all the beasts were gone, men would
die from a great loneliness of the spirit. For
whatever happens to the beasts soon happens to
man" (qtd. in Walter 40).

Wetlands, however, do more than protect
living plants and animals. They also work as so-
called "hydrologic modifiers," storing water and
then releasing it slowly, reducing the impact of
floods and droughts (Niering, "Swamp" 2). Because
giant parking lots, acres of buildings, masses of
concrete, and many square miles of pavement
literally waterproof the land, rainwater cannot
soak in; so it is concentrated in large run-offs.
Floods result. On the other hand, a one-acre swamp
with only a foot of water will retain 330,000
gallons. Thus, every time a wetland is destroyed,
the environment is dealt a double blow. First, the
the area's underground water supply diminishes;
and second, whatever water would have seeped into
the underground system increases area run-off,
thereby escalating downstream flooding (Goodwin
and Niering 7). As wetlands biologist Keith

Quotation marks
to indicate coined
word

Author cited in
text; need only
page number

For historical
perspective

Technical term
defined by
implication

Semicolon joining
two main clauses
including commas

Transitional
phrase

Single-word
transition

Transitional pair
to clarify effects

Blaser 8

Poole emphasized in a personal interview, "We
all live downstream."

The loss of wetlands also results in the
loss of nature's filtering systems. Wetlands
can remove sediments and pollutants like
giant kidneys (Niering, "Swamp" 2). They
sponge up pollutants such as the heavy metals
mercury and cadmium and agricultural run-off
like nitrogen, phosphorous, herbicides and
pesticides, consequently preventing these
toxic materials from flowing into fragile
estuaries and bays (Portal 12). In fact,
wetlands can even filter sewage. How? The
natural vegetation of a marsh, like cattails
and bulrushes, creates a natural fiber filter
"where microbes feed [on] nitrogen and
phosphorous, breaking them down to substances
readily absorbed by plants" (Klockenbrink
72). Then algae feed on whatever particles
are left while grasses function as a filter
for the clean water (Klockenbrink 72). In
reality, wetlands are so effective at
cleaning water that nearly 150 communities,
including San Diego and Disney World, use
artificial wetlands instead of traditional
sewage treatment plants. In so doing, they
reap a 50% to 90% savings (Brown 89; "Saving
Swamps" 45). The stream waters flowing out of
such wetlands are "cleaner than most
municipally treated water" and teem with
fish, and birds (Klockenbrink 72). To destroy
wetlands, then, is to remove nature's
kidneys. As Poole explained, "If you drink
water, you suffer" when wetlands are lost.

Complete in-text reference; no parenthetical citation neded

Topic sentence with transition; emphasizes effects

Transition emphasizing effects

Writer's substitution (source incorrectly used "off")

Two sentences (first a quotation); two citations

Combines information from two sources

Quotation and following verb phrase from same source

Personal interview needs no further documentation; refers to paragraph introduction

Blaser 9

Strangely enough, in spite of their sometimes vast watery expanses, wetlands also reduce storm damage by acting as buffers. ("Saving Swamps" 45). One writer gives this account:

> When Hurricane Hugo roared into South Carolina [in 1989], it smashed sea walls, ripped out dikes, and devastated an entire national forest. Yet, with the exception of some minor erosion caused mostly by man's compulsion to dredge channels where nature doesn't want them, the state's salt marshes went on quietly creating and recycling detritus and, in the process, feeding and sheltering a myriad of marine organisms. After Hugo, local shrimp production was as good as it gets. (Reiger 54)

Finally, wetlands also help maintain biospheric stability. Most important in the contribution to what circles the earth is the wetlands' role in producing oxygen (Niering, Wetlands 31-35). Scientific calculations indicate that, "512 acres [of wetlands] produce a net increase of twenty tons of oxygen per day" (Goodwin and Niering 5). That is no small impact in a world that justifiably worries about the greenhouse effect and the ozone layer.

The real problem, of course, is putting all these benefits in terms of dollars and cents. In an editorial, Peter A. A. Berle writes, "Economists still are not good at comparing the value of a wetlands ecosystem with that of a shopping-center parking lot..." (6). According to most authorities and as illustrated

---

Colon introduces long quotation (compare with earlier long quotation)

Writer adds date

Transition to conclude discussion of effects

Writer adds identifying phrase

Transitional sentence

Present tense

Ellipsis shows omission; final period after citation

Blaser 10

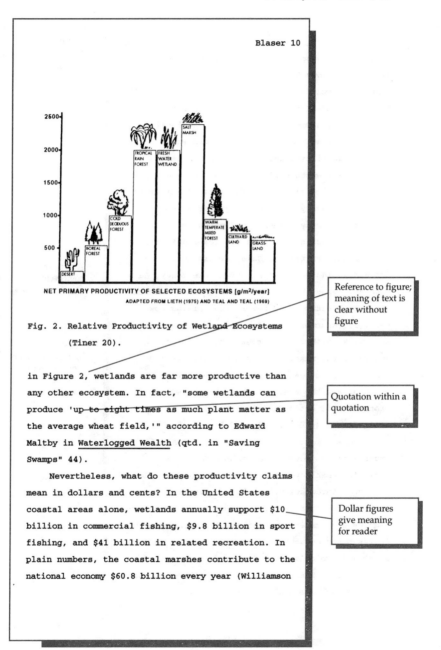

NET PRIMARY PRODUCTIVITY OF SELECTED ECOSYSTEMS [g/m²/year]
ADAPTED FROM LIETH (1975) AND TEAL AND TEAL (1969)

Fig. 2. Relative Productivity of Wetland Ecosystems
   (Tiner 20).

Reference to figure; meaning of text is clear without figure

in Figure 2, wetlands are far more productive than
any other ecosystem. In fact, "some wetlands can
produce 'up to eight times as much plant matter as
the average wheat field,'" according to Edward
Maltby in Waterlogged Wealth (qtd. in "Saving
Swamps" 44).

Quotation within a quotation

   Nevertheless, what do these productivity claims
mean in dollars and cents? In the United States
coastal areas alone, wetlands annually support $10
billion in commercial fishing, $9.8 billion in sport
fishing, and $41 billion in related recreation. In
plain numbers, the coastal marshes contribute to the
national economy $60.8 billion every year (Williamson

Dollar figures give meaning for reader

Blaser 11

42-43). In another example, annual productivity in
Georgia's Alcovy River Swamp exceeds values of
approximately $1.6 million for hardwood, $550,000
for fish, and $1 million for water quality—roughly
a $3.1 million impact each year to the local
Alcovy River economy (Goodwin and Niering 4-7).
When the statistics include indirect benefits,
wetlands are worth billions of dollars every year.

> Summary of statistics as conclusion

In spite of the many indicators of wetlands'
values, not everyone is willing to see the
benefits. In many communities, property owners
believe protecting wetlands stifles industrial
development (Portal 5). Some farmers still see
drained wetlands as a source for more money. As
with any issue, both sides express valid concerns.
Many earth citizens, however, are working toward
retaining what precious few wetlands remain. Ray
McCormick, an Indiana farmer honored for sound
environmental practices, used to drain wetlands as
a routine practice, but not anymore. "These
wetlands are the most valuable part of my farm.
Protection of wetlands is essential to
agriculture" (qtd. in Walter 27).

> Admission of controversy

> Hints at regulations; summarizes to maintain unity

Many earth citizens have joined dozens of
organizations, action groups, and research
societies that have as their goal to provide the
finances, information, and laws to protect wetlands
("There Are Other People"). Nevertheless, ignorance
remains the number one problem. In fact, wetlands
losses often occur when, according to Mary Kentula,
a wetland ecologist with Oregon State University,
someone fills land that "simply wasn't wet enough to
be recognized as a wetland" (Henahan 1).

Blaser 12

Shouldn't federal and state laws protect such
lands? As one critic lamented, "At best,
existing wetland laws and programs only slow
the rate of loss" because they are hard to
understand and harder still to enforce
(Baldwin 18).

More people are beginning to overcome the
chiller-movie image of wetlands and to
understand the importance of wetlands as
protectors. As Poole explained, "A hundred
years ago we could float down a river, drink
the water, and eat the fish without a second
thought. Not anymore. But if we can reclaim
the wetlands, we can clean up the rivers. And
if we don't there will be nothing left for
our children." If wetlands disappear, the
cost, both direct and indirect, is not just
in the billions of dollars; it is beyond
measure.

Reference to
introduction;
refernce to first
part of paper

Quotation to add
meaning to
"importance"

Reference to final
part of paper;
leaves reader with
serious thought

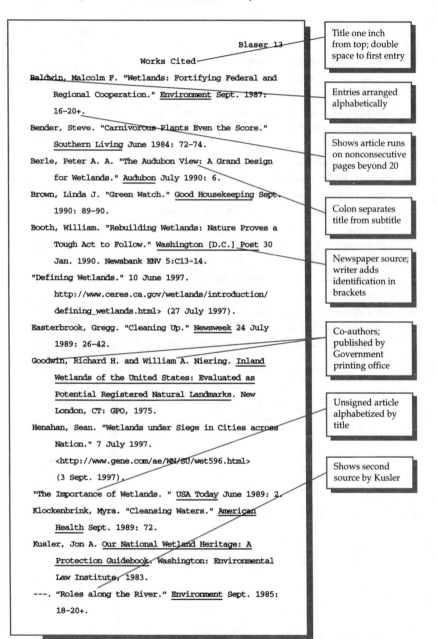

Blaser 13

Works Cited

Baldwin, Malcolm F. "Wetlands: Fortifying Federal and
Regional Cooperation." Environment Sept. 1987:
16-20+.

Bender, Steve. "Carnivorous Plants Even the Score."
Southern Living June 1984: 72-74.

Berle, Peter A. A. "The Audubon View: A Grand Design
for Wetlands." Audubon July 1990: 6.

Brown, Linda J. "Green Watch." Good Housekeeping Sept.
1990: 89-90.

Booth, William. "Rebuilding Wetlands: Nature Proves a
Tough Act to Follow." Washington [D.C.] Post 30
Jan. 1990. Newsbank ENV 5:C13-14.

"Defining Wetlands." 10 June 1997.
http://www.ceres.ca.gov/wetlands/introduction/
defining_wetlands.html> (27 July 1997).

Easterbrook, Gregg. "Cleaning Up." Newsweek 24 July
1989: 26-42.

Goodwin, Richard H. and William A. Niering. Inland
Wetlands of the United States: Evaluated as
Potential Registered Natural Landmarks. New
London, CT: GPO, 1975.

Henahan, Sean. "Wetlands under Siege in Cities across
Nation." 7 July 1997.
<http://www.gene.com/ae/WN/SU/wet596.html>
(3 Sept. 1997).

"The Importance of Wetlands. " USA Today June 1989: 2.

Klockenbrink, Myra. "Cleansing Waters." American
Health Sept. 1989: 72.

Kusler, Jon A. Our National Wetland Heritage: A
Protection Guidebook. Washington: Environmental
Law Institute, 1983.

---. "Roles along the River." Environment Sept. 1985:
18-20+.

Title one inch
from top; double
space to first entry

Entries arranged
alphabetically

Shows article runs
on nonconsecutive
pages beyond 20

Colon separates
title from subtitle

Newspaper source;
writer adds
identification in
brackets

Co-authors;
published by
Government
printing office

Unsigned article
alphabetized by
title

Shows second
source by Kusler

Blaser 14

Niering, William A. "Swamp, Marsh, and Bog." The New
    Grolier Electronic Encyclopedia. Danbury, CT:
    Publishing, Inc., 1988. CD-ROM

Wetlands: The Audubon Society Nature Guides. New
    York: Alfred A. Knopf, 1985.

Poole, Keith. Personal interview. 29 Jan. 1991.

Portal, Ann. "Wetlands: A Barrier to Growth?" The [Eugene,
    Oregon] Register Guard 20 Jan. 1990. Newsbank ENV
    15-D5.

Reiger, George. "Symbols of the Marsh." Audubon July 1990:
    52-58.

"Saving the Swamps." The Futurist Sept.-Oct. 1986: 44-45.

Sporre, Tom. "More Than Mosquitoes." Outdoor Indiana Nov.
    1990: 23-25.

Steinhart, Peter. "No Net Loss." Audubon July 1990: 18-21.

"There Are Other People Out There Who Care about
    Estuaries." Jan. 1997 <http://www. estuaries. org/
    links.html> (8 July 1997).

Tiner, Ralph W., Jr. Wetlands of the United States:
    Current Status and Recent Trends. Washington: Dept.
    of the Interior, Fish and Wildlife Service, 1984.

Walter, John. " Farming in the Flyways. " Successful
    Farming Feb. 1990: 25-37+.

"Wetlands Ducks: The Timeless Equation." Southern Living
    Nov. 1988: 62+

Williamson, Lonnie. "The Swampbusters." Outdoor Life Feb.
    1987: 42-43.

Computer data
source

Multiple sources
by same author
alphabetized
by title

Computer data
source

Unsigned Internet
Source

Government
publication

Compare Styles: MLA and APA

Some disciplines follow the *Publication Manual of the American Psychological Association* (APA) style for documentation. The following guidelines explain the differences between MLA and APA styles.

Parenthetical Citations

APA parenthetical citations follow this style:

- All parenthetical citations include the author's name and the date of publication.
- Page numbers are included only if reference is made in the paper to a specific page or chapter or if a quotation is included.
- When page numbers are included, they are preceded by the designation *p.* or *pp.*
- Items in the citation are separated by commas.

Examples:

(Norvell, 1992)
(Norvell, 1992, p. 16)
(Norvell, 1992, pp. 16-17)

Reference Pages

Instead of referring to a Works Cited page, the APA style uses the term Reference page. Still, the format is quite similar to MLA with the following exceptions:

- The date of publication follows, parenthetically, the author's name.
- Quotation marks are omitted from periodical article titles.

- Only first and proper words of titles are capitalized; the first word of a subtitle is not capitalized.

- Volume numbers of periodicals are underscored.

- Entries are double-spaced with hanging indentation, the second and subsequent lines being indented only three, rather than five, spaces.

Examples:

Carlson, Ruth Kearney. (1995, March). Poetry as a reading aid: an introduction. Elementary English, 62, 273-274.

Norvell, George W. (1990). The reading interests of young people. Boston: D.C. Heath and Company.

Use whichever style your teacher requests, and maintain consistency throughout your paper.